Speak Wιτn Impact

52 Speaking Tips For Women to Build Confidence, Clarity & Influence

Lisa V.

Your voice is an instrument of transformation.

LISA VANDERKWAAK

Lisa Vanderkwaak
REAL U Publishing & Media
Canada
www.LisaVanderkwaak.com

Ordering Information:
Quantity discounts are available on bulk purchases of this book for educational, gift purposes, or as premiums for increasing magazine subscriptions or renewals. For information, please contact Lisa Vanderkwaak at lisa@realu.ca .

A CIP record of this title is available from the Canadian Library and Archives

Speak With Impact
52 Speaking Tips for Women to Build Confidence, Clarity & Influence
$20.00
ISBN: 978-0-9958326-5-7
eBook ISBN: 978-0-9958326-6-4

Cover Photo by Lisa Leung Photography

Table of Contents

Introduction...vii

52 SPEAKING TIPS FOR WOMEN 1

   1. Find Your Voice...2

   2. Establish Foundations 4

CLARITY IS POWER 7

   3. Get Clear on Your Purpose and Your People 8

   4. Own Your Story 10

   5. Uncover Your Unique Life Message.................12

   6. Structure Your Message For Success 15

   7. Tune Up Your Message So Others Don't Tune Out..........17

   8. Don't Ride On Talent Alone 20

   9. Know Your Phase..23

CONFIDENCE..27

   10. Confidence Is Built Not Bought.....................28

   11. Flip the Switch on Fear 30

   12. Escape the Trap of Comparison 33

13. Don't Let Others Steal Your Confidence 36

14. Don't Throw Away Your Confidence 38

15. Practice Doesn't Always Make Perfect...........................40

16. Show up Prepared 42

CONTENT...**45**

17. Leverage Personal Experiences 46

18. Use Less Content For More Impact...............................48

19. Use the Power of Three...51

20. Make it Repeatable 52

21. Don't Retell a Story, Relive It.......................................54

22. Give Your Point a Story 56

23. Hook Your Audience Early 57

24. Pump Life into Your Message 59

25. It's What You Take Out of a Message That
Makes the Difference..61

26. Turn Your Content into a Keynote 63

AIM FOR CONNECTION NOT PERFECTION **67**

27. Go The Extra Mile With A Simple Smile 68

28. Connect With Your Audience Before You Speak............70

29. Build Trust Through Eye Contact...................................72

30. Look To All, Speak To One 73

31. Use You-Focused Language 76

32. Keep Them On the Edge of Their Seats 79

33. Don't Memorize, Internalize 81

34. Be Known As Similar, Not Special.................................. 83

35. Put First Things First 85

36. Share Your Accolades Authentically................................ 87

37. Think Like Your Audience.................................... 89

38. Be Aware of the Silent Killers 90

39. Reflection Makes A Deeper Connection 92

CLOSING WITH IMPACT **95**

40. Use Only One Exact Next Step.......................... 96

41. Make Your Points Stick.................................... 98

42. Make Your Message Memorable 100

43. A Shift in Perspective Can Make it More Effective....... 101

44. Last Impressions are Lasting Impressions 103

CAPTIVATING YOUR AUDIENCE **105**

45. Boost Your Confidence Daily 106

46. Write Your Own Introduction 109

47. Capture Audience Attention From The Start 111

48. Create Curiosity 114

49. How You Appear Can Draw Others Near 116

50. Don't Let Side-Bars Become Slide-Bars 118

51. Use Powerpoint Only If Necessary 120

52. Your Delivery Will Determine Your Impact 123

BONUS TIP: Value Progress Over Perfection 125

About The Author 127

Introduction

ave you ever wondered what makes some women better speakers than others? You may be like most women and disqualify yourself believing you are not naturally talented or don't have what it takes to become a transformational speaker. I know I believed those lies at one time, until I discovered that effectiveness in public speaking is not so much based on talent, but rather on skill development. That is, over 90% of effective communication is because the speaker took time to invest in learning proven ways to structure their message and in developing the skills needed to deliver a clear, concise compelling message.

There is a global demand for women speakers who are highly skilled in communication, and in particular, who can stand with confidence, deliver a strong message and motivate audiences to action.

You *can* start developing these skills if you are willing to learn and put into practice the tips and tools contained within this book. I know, because these tips are some of the tools that helped me do the same. I used to be so scared of public speaking that I remember shaking in my boots. My heart would be racing and my vocal cords felt paralyzed at the mere thought of having to participate in a small group discussion.

After falling flat on my face as an aspiring speaker, I spent the past 3 decades learning what I could to become a more effective communicator. As a result, I have had the privilege of being coached by some of the best speakers in the world and glean from their experience and wisdom. Today I have a passion to help other women find their voice, and become free to offer their unique contribution to the world through speaking. I want to dispel the myths around what it takes to not only deliver a clear, compelling message with impact, but also about creating wealth doing what you are uniquely called to do. By learning how to use speaking to expand your income will open up opportunities to have a much wider impact on the world around you.

I never considered myself someone who loved to talk. In fact, for many years, I did not have a voice. Throughout my childhood, I lived through many painful and confusing experiences that led me to believe that it is safer to be silent. It was only when I was in my early twenties, after walking through a journey of personal transformation, that I rediscovered my voice and my courage to speak again emerged. I have met many women who have been held back from sharing their story because of fear and limiting beliefs. Many have lost their voice and actually believe they don't have what it takes to become a great communicator. Perhaps you can relate?

I am so glad you picked up this book because I am on a mission to dispel that myth. You do have what it takes *and* your voice is meant to be heard.

In the following chapters, you will discover that you are created to speak, it is part of your DNA. You will also pick up valuable and practical tools to apply immediately as you develop the skills that will enable you to speak with transformational impact. By implementing these 52 tips, one a week, you will see a noticeable difference in your confidence, clarity and impact as a communicator. However, I am also interested in something deeper happening as you engage with what you learn in this book. I pray that you gain the personal freedom to express your unique story and experience the joy of fulfilling your unique purpose. In addition, I hope that you come to understand the importance of investing in improving your speaking skills and why staying the same is no longer an option.

I invite you to explore the possibility that you were given a voice to use, and learning how to use it with love, integrity, and skill will allow you to have a far greater impact than you thought possible.

Why am I writing these for women? Well, the truth is that I can't get away from the sense that God is wanting to release women to a whole new level of freedom and restoring the power of your voice is part of that. How I do that is by sharing my story and the foundational truths that helped me find my voice, own my story and move forward in freedom, courage and conviction to speak the truth in the spheres of influence I find myself. By implementing these 52 transformational speaking tips you will shortcut your learning and save yourself a lot of headaches and avoid embarrassing mistakes.

The other reason why I am writing this for women is because of the increased demand for women speakers around the globe. Many women speakers believe that just because they have no problem speaking in front of groups that they must be a great speaker. However, there is so much more to it than that. Little do they know that to become a great speaker, it is important to realize that public speaking is less about what you have to give and more about what the audience gets. It is not so much about conveying information as it is about *evoking transformation* in the hearts and minds of those who are listening.

To speak with impact will first of all require you to embrace transformation at a personal level. Then you will be required to embrace a growth mindset in order to learn how to create and deliver a clear, concise, and compelling message. As well, you will need to develop the skills and confidence to own the stage and give a strong call to action.

The following 52 speaking tips are divided into sections so you can take one tip a week and implement it right away into new messages you are creating. When you do, At the end of one year, you will see significant improvements in your confidence, clarity and speaking impact. The speed of implementation is key to seeing results and growth. Test, tweak, and then master them. The tips are not organized in any order of importance but according to categories. My desire is that these tools will serve as building blocks for you to be able to own your story, learn how to turn your mess into a powerful message and develop the skills to speak in such a way that lives and lifestyles are transformed.

I would love to hear from you after a few months of applying the tips, and again after one year of implementing them, to hear about your journey of becoming a transformational speaker.

For a more enriched learning experience, I encourage you to subscribe to my youtube channel: www.LisaV.tv

52 SPEAKING TIPS FOR WOMEN

Getting Started

1.

Find Your Voice

Have you ever found yourself in a situation where you really wanted to do something but just felt stuck, held back and didn't really know why?

I found myself in that place back in my twenties when I was at a banquet for a group of people who had just graduated from a course that my late husband and I had taught over a series of weeks. So, here we are at this banquet and my husband is giving a speech and then he turns to me and asks me to say a few words.

If you had been standing next to me that day, you would have seen my face and neck turn beet red and my eyes start to scan the room for a way of escape. What you would not have noticed is that even though my body and mind were protesting that day, my heart was actually yearning to be able to say something that made a difference in the lives of those students. That was the day I decided I needed to get unstuck, and the first thing I needed to do was to find my voice.

I knew where I had lost it. I was 7 years old, standing at the foot of a hospital bed staring at this woman who was laying there with a face that was so badly bruised and swollen, that she was unrecognizable. I stood there frozen with fear. Then she spoke. If it had not been for her familiar voice, I would not have believed that it was my mom. You see, my dad was a wife beater and often when my mom spoke he would react in anger. That day I decided it wasn't safe to speak. That was the day I lost my voice.

So fast-forward to the banquet. I knew when I had lost it, I just didn't know how to get it back. That led me on a quest to seek out help from other women who were doing what I wanted to do. The truths they taught me came alive in me. Along the way, over a number of years, I had other mentors and coaches who each deposited something in me that helped me own who I was as a person, and the steps I needed to take to get unstuck in this area and move forward. What I learned from each of them changed the way I saw public speaking and ultimately shifted the course of my life. I discovered that I am created for a unique purpose and that my story matters and that my voice is an important part of my unique contribution to the world.

Just as this is true for me, it is true for you too!

The road to freedom and speaking with impact, starts with finding your voice. Do you know where you lost yours?

Like me, the process of regaining your voice may include embracing.

Emotional

And spiritual transformation and extending forgiveness to some people in your life, past and present.

Your voice is part of your unique contribution you are meant to give to the world. It's time to speak!

Application:

Have you lost your voice? What do you need to do to get it back?

2.

⚭

Establish Foundations

With the invention of the internet and the rapid evolution of video technology, you no longer have any excuse to not start speaking. Anywhere, any time, you can be in front of your ideal audience around the world with the simple click of a button on your mobile device.

To get started as a speaker and to continue growing in effectiveness you will need to establish three essential pillars. These pillars form a strong foundation upon which all other aspects of public speaking rest. Each of these pillars will be discussed in greater detail in later sections.

Here's a brief description of each for your consideration:

1. *Your Story.* Do you know what your life message is and how to communicate it? What is your unique life story?
2. *Skills.* What skills do you need so you can create and deliver a clear, concise message? Have you developed the skills to keep your audience engaged from start to finish?
3. *Systems.* Knowing how to choose the right amount of content, and how to organize it into a structure and sequence that is clear and concise is essential. There are proven systems that can help you do just that, as well as, help you learn how to create wealth by getting paid for

your unique ideas, experiences, and expertise. Evaluate where you are at in your speaking ability and determine what systems you need to learn first in order to expand your capacity to speak with impact and go to the next level in effectiveness. To help you get started take the free assessment tool at lisavanderkwaak.com/msc-tool.

Application:

How can you establish a stronger foundation as you continue to develop as a public speaker? What pillar do you need to strengthen and focus on first?

Clarity is Power

"Without a vision, people wander aimlessly."

3.

∽

Get Clear on Your Purpose and Your People

What motivates you to want to be a speaker? Is it that you want to inspire people with your story? Or do you simply "love the attention"? Have you learned a few things through your experiences and education and you feel compelled to pass these learnings on to others? Perhaps you realize that improvements in your communication skills will increase your chances of advancements in your career or lead to higher paying positions. Research confirms that women who are skilled in communication get more job promotions, get paid more, are viewed as more credible, and experience higher levels of success in their field of interest.

Public speaking skills are so important that many companies are providing mandatory communication training to their staff. According to business magnate, Warren Buffett, investing in developing your public speaking skills can potentially lead to increasing your net worth by about fifty percent. Of all the entrepreneurs I have met over the years, the most successful ones all attribute their success to taking time to improve their public speaking skills and incorporating speaking into their business model.

Perhaps it has nothing to do with your job but just a burning desire inside you to make a difference in people's lives. Speaking is the best way to increase your influence and impact. Getting clear on your purpose is the first step to speaking with impact. If you're not clear, your audience won't be either.

Do you have a story that needs to be told? Do you have a solution to a problem that people need? Have you experienced victory over an area of life that you want to share with others who are struggling to help them overcome?

Application:

Take time to get clear on your purpose, and on the people that you want to reach.

4.

⚭

Own Your Story

If someone called tomorrow to ask you to fill in for them at a speaking engagement, what would you do? Would you be ready with a message? Whether you are speaking for free or fee there are some things you can do today to prepare for such opportunities, and be ready to speak at a moment's notice. I have developed a 6 step process called the *S.M.I.L.E.S. Formula™* that helps people to prepare to speak and adapt their message to the time and audience. One of the key elements of this process is developing what is known as your *life message* or a *unique signature message™*.

Did you know that our DNA is 98% the same? It's the 2% of your DNA code that makes up your uniqueness,

Since the 1970's, Geneticists have been converting the long strands of DNA code into sound. By assigning musical pitches to the 22 combinations of amino acids they discovered that it was easier to detect differences in musical sequences than in analyzing the raw scientific data. The format has allowed them to compare DNA, look for mutations, then reverse engineer the amino acids back into proteins. This discovery opened the way for musical scientists to develop the system further. Today, DNA music is being taken seriously by composers and including DNA sequences into songs.

Dan McCollam, a pastor in California shared a story about the father of a family who decided he was going to send the DNA of all of his children and he and his wife to a certain composer who could convert the DNA into music as a gift.

The family had a piano in the home and every time the 6 year old son would go by the piano, he would play the same sequence of notes. Apparently, he wasn't taking music lessons and it was always the same combination without fail every time he passed by the piano. To the family's surprise, when they received the songs from the composer, the one converted from the boy's DNA code included the exact same sequence of notes that the boy played on the piano. The composer had no prior knowledge of the little boys favorite sequence of notes. He just strictly composed the song that corresponded to the boy's DNA. So what does that mean? That little boy's *life song* was trying to get out, to get expressed.

I believe that just like we all have a unique life song, we also all have a *life message* that needs to be expressed. What is the unique story or message inside of you that needs to come out?

That needs to be heard? The first step to expressing it is embracing and owning it as your unique contribution to the world.

I believe that until you take steps to regain your voice and own your life story you will never be truly fulfilled.

At this point you may be thinking, "But I have a lot of stories, which one is my life message." That is a struggle many women have. How do you know which one to start with? The next tip will help you uncover your unique message and give you a framework to get started.

Application:

Make a decision today to own your life story

5.

⤬

Uncover Your Unique Life Message

If you are like me, you may have a lot of stories throughout your life of struggle and overcoming. It can be overwhelming to know where to start. You want to avoid the mistake many speakers make in giving too much content in their message and leaving their audience overwhelmed.

One of the ways you can begin to express your life story or message is through a *Unique Signature Message (USM™)*. This is a talk or presentation that is based on a topic that you are passionate about, contains a part of your story of overcoming that can be used to help others. Depending on the purpose of your message and the people you are reaching, you may use a USM or a shorter version, called a testimony, that serves to introduce you to a new audience and build trust and credibility. It helps them understand who you are, what you are all about and why you do what you do.

Your opening statements are important to capture your audience's attention and establish trust. After outlining what they will be learning you will want to tell them about yourself through the use of a story or statement that includes an element of vulnerability. The essence of your signature message will stay the same however how you say it may vary as you keep growing it and learning various ways to express it. You have a unique purpose on the earth and by identifying and sharing your unique message you will find yourself walking more consistently in that purpose.

Remember, being a speaker is not about saying it *perfectly* but more about speaking *purposefully.*

As you function in your unique gifts and purpose you cause the people around you to grow and rise up to function in theirs.

Here's a simple exercise to help you uncover a topic for your USM:

1. Write out some of the topics that you are passionate about and would love to speak about. Even if you don't have all the content figured out, just start making a list.
2. Ask yourself these questions:

Q. If you had an opportunity to speak to a group on whatever you wanted, what is the first topic you would choose?

Q. How would you want that audience to think, feel and act after hearing your message?

Q. What transformation would you like the audience members to walk away with? How would you like their lives to be different as a result of hearing you speak?

Q. What qualifies you to speak on that topic?

Q. What were the experiences you had related to the topic that others can learn from?

Do you believe that you are created for a unique purpose? In fact, your ability to embrace that truth will significantly affect your confidence as a speaker. This uniqueness is like your personal brand and needs to be expressed in a way that reaches the right people.

Application:

Answer the above questions to uncover your unique message that you are meant to bring to the world.

6.

⊸⊱⊰⊶

Structure Your Message For Success

Whether it involves planning your day, a vacation, or having a vision for your future, being clear about what you want and where you are going is a powerful tool to increase productivity. The same is true for public speaking. If you are clear about your message, then your audience will be too. The clearer you express that message, the more likely that your listeners will stay engaged and be impacted. After you decide on the topic for your first USM, next the content needs to be converted into a format, so you express it in a way others can receive it.

To create clear, concise and compelling messages takes skill and having a proven structure will help facilitate this goal. Knowing how to organize your information into a clear structure is key! This is so important that I developed a whole course on the exact structure I use that allows me to adapt my message to any audience, and any time frame. If you are interested in going deeper in learning the exact proven method of creating your Unique Signature Message™ that is used by the most successful speakers, and want to learn how to use speaking to increase your influence, impact and income, check out

EmergingWomenSpeakers.com for training details.

If your audience can follow what you are saying, they will remember it better and are more apt to stay engaged. Having a clear structure has many benefits. Here are just a few:

1. Acts as a guide so you don't have to refer to your notes as often.
2. Keeps your audience engaged longer.
3. Increases clarity and focus to help people move forward or make a change.
4. Makes your message memorable and stick in people's minds long after you finish speaking.

Application:

Seek out a speaking coach or a program like my *Profitable Talks Formula*™ to learn a proven method of structuring your message for success.

7.

⌒∞⌒

Tune Up Your Message So Others Don't Tune Out

Have you ever heard a speaker and wondered what exactly they were trying to say? Perhaps they were all over the place, stringing stories and statements together that were interesting but had no obvious relation to each other.

Most speakers don't realize that it is not just what you say but *how* you say it that makes a message most impactful. Among other things, it's the way you structure your message, make deep and meaningful connections, and leave your audience members feeling empowered and transformed. There are certain skills that make the best speakers stand out from the rest. Taking the time to develop these skills will give you the opportunity to become the kind of speaker whose influence lasts long after you leave the stage.

Skilled public speakers know that less is actually more when it comes to how much information you give your audience.

Especially when it relates to how much time should you spend on emphasizing each point, having a proven structure is key.

Here is one example of a simple formula to follow:

Make a point, tell a story. Make another point, tell another story.

However, most speakers only do this and give too much content, therefore saturating the message. The most effective way to make a point is to give not several stories but one story per point, or one example per point. Unless of course you are wanting to really emphasize a point to give different perspectives on it.

Too many stories can overwhelm your audience and actually deprive them of learning more. When preparing your message, consider the element of quantity. Namely, how many points will you make, how many stories will you tell, how much information will you give your audience. How much is enough and how much is too much? These elements are discussed in more detail in other sections.

To get a clear message, you may need to sort through your ideas and lay aside those that only serve to distract or clutter your message. If the content doesn't enhance your point, exclude it. Include enough to make your point and resist the urge to give them everything you know on that topic.

Take the time to *tune up your message so others don't tune out* when you are speaking. A clear message sticks longer in people's minds and has a greater potential for impact. Having a proven structure to use over and over helps you create a message easier and acts as a framework to keep it concise and compelling.

Application:

Here's another few simple structures to get started in creating a clear Signature Message.

A) Story-Struggle-Solution

Share a Story

Tell what the Struggle was

Reveal the Solution of how you overcame the struggle.

B) Heart-Head-Hands-Heart (I got this from Ed Tate)

Heart - Share a story

Head- give main points

Hands- Practical tips

Heart - How this related to listener

8.

❧

Don't Ride On Talent Alone

D o you know someone who is a natural born storyteller? Do you believe you could never tell stories like her/ him? Several years ago, I had an "aha" moment while attending a coach training. I realized that deep down I *believed* that "I am **not** a natural-born storyteller" and used that as an excuse to not incorporate more stories into my messages. That day I stepped out of my comfort zone and got coached on how to become a more effective storyteller. As I learned some simple techniques and tools I became more confident in storytelling. I also realized that even if I wasn't a *natural-born* storyteller I could still *learn the skills* and increase my impact as a speaker. The key was being coachable and not letting the limiting beliefs hold me back. I started to get excited as I applied the secrets of storytelling and saw how much more the audience stayed engaged when I spoke.

Craig Valentine told a story of when he first started learning about public speaking, he entered the humorous speech contest at his local Toastmasters chapter and lost. At the end of the evening a gentleman approached Craig and said, "Craig, you could win the world championship of public speaking." Craig looked at him confused and said something like, "Buddy, I just lost the humorous speech contest at the club level." The man responded and said, "I know. The only thing that was wrong with your humorous speech is that it wasn't funny!"

Then he said something that helped shift Craig's mindset. He told Craig that he believed that if he intentionally focused on improving his skills, he could win the world's speech contest. Craig took his words to heart, hired a speaking coach, and in that same year, 1999, went on to win the World Championship of Public Speaking.

What was that gentleman doing? He observed that Craig had a natural talent for public speaking, but he also knew that Craig would only go so far if he didn't develop the necessary skills to take him to the next level.

Research has confirmed this fact as findings show that people who are naturally gifted in an area, such as sports for example, will only go so far on talent alone. Those who are less talented but who have intentionally invested in developing supporting skills end up going farther in that area than those who started out with more talent.

Many women disqualify themselves because of lack of natural talent. I know I was one of them. You may have a similar belief about speaking in general, and are telling yourself, "I am not a gifted speaker." What you believe may be limiting you. The good news is that you don't have to be a natural-born communicator to be effective; all you need is the following to break through and move you forward with confidence.

1. *Acknowledge* that you have a desire to become a positive voice of influence.
2. *Believe* that you can become an effective speaker and embrace a growth mindset by being coachable.

3. *Commit* to the process by immediately putting into practice whatever you learn as you step out of your comfort zone. The more you implement your learnings the more your confidence will grow.

Application:

Apply the above 3 steps and identify one thing you need to do to increase your impact as a speaker.

9.

⹎⹎⹎

Know Your Phase

Whether you are a novice or experienced speaker you can expect to go through stages of development as you grow in confidence and fine-tune your speaking skills. According to David Brooks, 1990 World Champion of Public Speaking, there are at least 3 phases or stages. I have taken his ideas and expanded them to 5 phases. See if you can identify what phase of development you're in as a speaker.

Phase one is where everyone starts. During this phase you are most concerned about yourself. How you appear to your audience, whether they like you. You are focused on saying the right words at the right time. Most women speakers stay in this phase and because they get comfortable speaking in front of people and maybe get a few laughs, they think they are "good" at public speaking. And they are probably right.

However, "good" speakers don't make huge impact long term and don't get higher paying speaking gigs like the "great" speakers get. Historically, this has been true especially for women speakers. The question you need to answer is "Do you want to be a good speaker or a great speaker?" Do you want to do what most speakers do or stand out by doing what masterful speakers do? If you want to grow then don't settle and stay at this phase.

Phase one is all about preparation and getting clear on your message, your audience and purpose. You may be speaking occasionally and even feel like you're good at it. But don't stop there. Keep developing as a speaker.

Phase two is when you become more concerned about the message and how others perceive you. I call it the *Positioning Phase*. It's an important phase to establish your trust and credibility and get clear on what you stand for. However, you may also be focused on getting it perfect. This is where most speakers stop and settle.

Focusing on perfection is one of the biggest hindrances to connecting deeply with your audience.

Instead of perfection focus on connection and take the time to invest in developing the skills to more effectively engage your audience and keep them on the edge of their seats wanting more.

This is when move into phase three, you understand that speaking is not so much about what you have to give but more about what your audience takes away. To reiterate, good speakers are comfortable with themselves, and with their message, but great speakers are most concerned with their audiences. Great speakers have learned that to be a transformational speaker you need to make your audience your main concern. At this stage, you focus on not just communicating but *connecting* in meaningful ways to your audience, intellectually, emotionally and even spiritually.

This is called the *Personal Impact Phase*. This is also the phase where your personal development goes to a whole new level – if you allow it. To become the kind of speaker that has a transformational impact on your audience members, you need to first commit to the process of transformation in your own life. In my experience, this is a pivotal phase. The degree to which you develop the ability to make a lasting impact on people's lives is the degree to which you'll succeed as a speaker.

The final two phases are the *Profit Phase* and *Platform Development Phase*. Unfortunately, most speakers start at these phases first. They seek to get speaking gigs before getting clear on their message or before gaining credibility. If you do this, before long you'll realize you have gaps in your public speaking effectiveness and have to circle back to strengthen the foundations you missed.

It doesn't matter in which phase you find yourself as long as you are aware of it and know what to do to eventually move to the next phase in your development as a speaker.

If you desire to have the impact of a transformational speaker then you may discover that having a speaking coach somewhere along the journey will be a tremendous asset.

Ken Blanchard, author of *The One Minute Manager*, reminds us that,

"Most highly successful athletes hire not one, but several coaches, each with specialized training expertise and perspectives. They use their coaches' feedback to create a performance benchmark against which they monitor progress and change. Their coaches make the difference between their success and failure."

I'm so glad I've had great mentors and coaches in my life who dared to tell me the truth and hold me accountable to keep stretching beyond my comfort zone to new levels of greatness. If you are serious about growing in confidence and competence in public speaking then you'll be thrilled with the tools, techniques and valuable keys taught at the Emerging Women Speakers Academy. If you want to understand more about the 5 Phases of Speaker Development and what you need to progress to the next level, you can download the FREE PDF booklet at www. LisaVanderkwaak.com/phases.

Application:

Determine what development phase you're in as a speaker. Find a mentor or speaking coach to help you create a strategy to get you to the next stage.

Confidence

10.

∽

Confidence Is Built Not Bought

onfidence is what fuels us to action and your actions lead to even greater confidence. They work hand in hand to move you forward, The Apostle Paul urges, "Do not throw away your confidence which has a great reward"(Heb 10:35).

Confidence is a vital key in moving forward in any area of life. You may be like most people and have at one time, disqualified yourself from ever becoming a great speaker because of a seemingly lack of confidence. Feeling discomfort, fear and anxiety concerning the unknown may immobilize you when faced with opportunities to do what you really want to do, such as share your expertise or experience. The presence of fear and discomfort are not always indicators that you shouldn't or can't do something. They are merely signals to examine in order to understand the limiting beliefs that may be keeping you stuck. The late Jay Conrad Levinson, marketing expert, once said that, "Confidence is the number one reason why people do business with you."

People are attracted to strength. People want to follow leaders who exhibit strength of character and confidence. Best-selling author and coach, Valorie Burton, says that the most successful women know what they can offer to the world and what skills they still need to develop.

Speaking with confidence expands your ability to influence and impact. Being comfortable in your own skin and embracing your unique qualities are important steps to building your confidence. You can't *buy* more confidence, but you can invest in *building* your confidence. The fact that you are reading this book shows that you are serious about personal development and want to offer your best self to the world. Congratulations on taking this first step towards building your self-confidence as a public speaker.

From as young as I can remember, I was ruled by fears of many kinds, which caused me to become extremely anxious even if I had to speak in a small group discussion. Confidence was not something I was born with, but something that was built over a process of learning, risking and being encouraged to step out of my comfort zone- which I am continuing to do so, even many years later. Author and business psychologist, Larina Kase, developed a growth process to help leaders push past their anxiety and fear to a place of confidence. You will learn more about this strategy in the next section.

The first stage in growth is in building confidence. The word "confidence" comes from the root word that means "with faith" or "with trust." Do you have faith that your story or message needs to be heard? Do you have an inner knowing that *you* are called to speak? Do you trust that someone is waiting (and needs) to hear what you have to share? Trust and faith both require taking a risk. Where do you find your confidence is most often attacked? What are the thoughts that rush through your mind when faced with a decision to step forward out of your comfort zone?

11.

❧

Flip the Switch on Fear

It's no secret that public speaking is said to be the number one fear among humans. What most people don't realize is that fear, however, can be harnessed and used towards positive outcomes. Even seasoned speakers experience anxiety and fear to some degree. The difference is that they confront and harness the energy to move them forward. The chemical reactions from fear and excitement are released for the same part in the brain. You can flip the switch on fear by replacing the thoughts you are having with positive ones. Instead of focusing on what you don't want to happen, focus on what you do want and this can help the shift the energy from fear to excitement. Instead of focusing on overcoming fear, I help my clients shift their focus to building confidence and in the process the fear dissipates.

The important question to ask yourself is:

Are you taking intentional steps to increase your confidence as a speaker?

Are you ready to start learning the necessary skills to speak with greater impact?

You will see a significant change in your effectiveness as a speaker, when you take these deliberate steps to build your confidence and gain clarity. This strategy contains a combination of my own steps and some picked up from Larina Kase. These are my 7 P's to Building Confidence as a Speaker.

1. Design a personal growth plan. Your growth as an individual will have a direct impact on your success in every area of life. Taking time to reflect and assess where you need to grow personally is not only wise but essential. Most people are held back because of issues of the heart that are unresolved or mindsets that keep them stuck. Showing up as authentic, the real you, will be the biggest attraction factor.

2. Identify your passion points. Taking time to identify topics that you are most passionate about and have the most experience with will help build your confidence. Starting with these topics as a speaker will help you to show up in strength, leading your audience to develop trust and credibility more quickly.

3. Start with the people who are within your immediate sphere of influence and who already see you as credible. Who are the people that already know you and are your raving fans?

4. Preparation. Being prepared is one of the simplest, most effective ways, to build your confidence. Many speakers wing it far too often and soon discover that such a habit eventually chips away at their confidence. Also, it often affects the audience's level of trust and engagement. The best speakers who tend to be able to speak "off the cuff", are usually the most prepared. An ancient proverb attributes preparation to the success of the ant. The proverb goes like this: "Ants aren't strong but they store up food all summer." The ants are considered one of the top four things on earth that are small but unusually wise because of their diligence to prepare.

5. Track your Progress. Focus on progress not perfection. Set yourself "stretch goals", ones that stretch you beyond your comfort zone. Whenever you step out of your comfort zone you will experience anxiety and if you keep stepping forward you will experience the greatest growth, compared to staying where you are. The reality is that a certain amount of discomfort is necessary if you are to succeed. There is good and bad anxiety. Paying attention to the signals you get is important.

6. Practice your message. Practice alone will not increase your effectiveness. Practicing the right habits will pay off in dividends. Ask a skilled speaker or speaking coach to give you feedback on your delivery as to any bad habits that are hindering your success.

7. Prayer. This last step acknowledges that transformation is not achieved by mere words alone. It takes a supernatural intervention to create lasting change. Taking time to pray acknowledges that you believe that human effort alone accomplishes nothing. When you pray, you are asking God to infuse your words with his power, so the impact will go beyond the natural to supernatural. That's the path of transformation. Commit your ways to God and he will make your path straight.

Application:

Invest in your personal development by following the above 7 steps to building your confidence.

12.

∽

Escape the Trap of Comparison

D id you know that the most valuable asset you carry is *You*? Audiences are most attracted to people who are real and authentic. As a speaker you may be tempted to imitate other people's style or method because of their success. However, I want to caution you that when you learn from other speakers, take what is useful and adapt it to fit your own personality and uniqueness.

Avoid comparing yourself to others, and instead learn to measure your success in the following three ways:

1) **By your level of fulfillment**. Success means different things to different people. I believe that successful people are not always fulfilled, but fulfilled people usually enjoy feelings of success. What is your definition of success? If it involves others then it will be short-lived and unsatisfactory. Define what success looks like for you. Does it align with what you sense is the divine purpose you have on the earth? Dig deep and get clear on what will truly make you feel most fulfilled.

2) **By your growth**. If you are constantly growing and can identify definite improvements, changes or learnings since 6 or 12 months ago, then you are moving forward. Staying

at the same place for too long can cause stagnation and even setbacks. Set a plan of action to continue growing and sharpening your speaking skills and compare your progress against where you were 1 year ago to where you are today. This will be a truer measure of success.

3) **By how authentic you are**. How true are you living to your own values and purpose? Embracing the process of becoming freer to live from your authentic place, and truer to your core purpose brings lasting change and fulfillment. Audiences want to see the real you and it can potentially be the most impactful!

Measuring your success by your own progress and not comparing yourself to others will cause your confidence to soar much faster.

No matter what your experience or expertise, the greatest asset you have to offer is you! Applying the tools and developing the skills to become an effective speaker is only half the equation. You must embrace who you are and learn to express yourself in such a way that reflects your authentic self. You carry a unique combination that the world is waiting to receive and learn from. This combination consists of your experiences, strengths, passions, personal struggles and triumph, and your true self. This is the unique offering you bring! When you seek to become who you are designed to be, there is no room for comparison nor perfection, only honest reflection of who you really are! As you continue to move forward in practicing your speaking skills, keep in mind what writer,

Anna Quinlan said:

"The thing that is really hard, and really amazing, is giving up on being perfect and beginning the work of becoming yourself."

13.

⤸⤸

Don't Let Others Steal Your Confidence

T he next few tips will list some of the most common ways that your confidence may become hijacked. Becoming aware of these confidence stealers will help you avoid them.

The most common way that confidence can be stolen is through believing other people's opinions. Do you know a negative person? How does it make you feel when you are around them? To continue to build confidence and move towards realizing your dream of becoming an effective speaker, you will need to make some hard choices and brave actions. Some people in our life will never be encouraging or happy for us, no matter what we do. It's important to identify the people in your life who could potentially steal your confidence with their words and opinions. Then make a decision to limit your interactions with the boundaries around the conversation. It's possible to hear what others have to say, love them, yet agree to disagree. It's your responsibility to filter what others say about you through the grid of God's truth and His unique purpose for your life. Recognize that your journey will look different than someone else's because of the process and preparation you need to go through to become free to live the real you fully.

If you struggle with letting other people's opinions influence your thinking and behaviour, then I invite you to explore whether you still have unresolved issues from your past or struggle with intimidation, fear of rejection or fear of people's approval. Until you are completely free from these fears, your confidence will be sabotaged over and over. As the ancient Hebrew proverb says, fearing people's opinion of you is a dangerous trap, but trusting in God's truth will bring you safety (Proverb 29:25).

Application:

List the people whose opinions have been stealing your confidence.

Decide what you will do to avoid this from happening.

Decide to establish your confidence on God's truth about you. Journal about it.

14.

❦

Don't Throw Away Your Confidence

W e can be our own worst critic and be constantly shooting ourselves down before we even get started. It's the thoughts that rush through your mind, trying to sabotage your success that leave you shipwrecked in your confidence, if you believe them to be true. When I first starting speaking I had to constantly battle the thoughts in my head that said, "who do you think you are?" and "what makes you think these people want to listen to you?". Thankfully, along the way I had mentors who taught me that my perceptions may not always be accurate, and if left unchallenged my perception can lead to deception.

At every stage of your life, you'll need to align yourself with wise people who can help guide you along in the direction of re-orienting your life to God's truth about you. Especially when you trip up or fail, you'll need someone to call upon to help you gain perspective and instead of giving up, get up and use it as an opportunity to gain new insights and grow as you keep moving forward.

As mentioned previously, there's a passage in the Christian Bible that says; "Don't throw away your confidence (in God), for it comes with a rich reward" (Heb 10:35). Whatever you are called to do, God will empower you to do it as you trust more in His ability to empower you instead of looking at your lack of ability.

Who can you call upon to help you overcome the self-talk that may be holding you back?

What truth in God's Word can you declare to overcome the limiting beliefs?

How can you protect your confidence from the the negative self-talk?

Application:

Be proactive and write out two statements of truth to combat each lie of self-talk that tries to sabotage you.

15.

❦

Practice Doesn't Always Make Perfect

H ave you ever heard the saying, "Practice makes perfect"? Well, it's not exactly true. Practice doesn't always lead to doing something perfectly, especially if you are practicing wrong habits. Yes, practice is an important part of fine-tuning your speaking skills. Therefore, the first step is to become aware of any bad habits you have in the area of public speaking.

When I was a teenager I learned how to dance ballet from books that had visuals of ballet poses and watching dancers on television. My family couldn't afford to pay for formal lessons so I practiced what I learned and would spend hours practicing in my family's living room. It was not until I went to university and enrolled in formal ballet classes that I discovered that much of what I had been practicing were not accurate. My instructor first had to help me unlearn the bad habits before I could master the good habits.

How will you know if you are practicing the wrong habits? The easiest way is to video record yourself speaking and then play it back to observe not only what you say but how you say it including your body movements and non-verbal language.

Another way is to ask someone for honest feedback after you speak. Don't just anyone, ask someone who is skilled in public speaking and can actually give you helpful tips. This is where a certified speaking coach comes in. No successful person got there on their own. A mistake that emerging speakers make is that they ask their friends or people who themselves are not skilled speakers and therefore do not always get helpful feedback.

Leadership expert, Peter Drucker once said; "Feedback is the breakfast of champions."

Mastering a skill takes time (10,000 hours to exact), lots of practice and fine-tuning.

Application:

Commit to the process of ongoing growth and be open to honest evaluations along the way from competent people who can help you become aware of bad habits and replace them with good habits that take you to the next level in effectiveness.

16.

⚬∞⚬

Show up Prepared

We live in a visually stimulating, fast-paced world that tries to engage us at every turn. The pitfall of overstimulation is that it can lead to shallow communication and surface relationships. I have noticed that most people go through life just getting by and living in reaction mode. To build your confidence as a speaker, you need to resist the urge to just throw something together to say. As mentioned earlier, speaking is not so much about what you have to say as it is about what your audience will take away. Randomly picking content and slapping it together to make a message or winging it will eventually work against you. Having a clear focus nurtures confidence and frees you to give of yourself when you speak.

When you take the time to carefully prepare your message, you will gain clarity and in turn feed your confidence at the time of delivery.

Here are three questions to ask yourself as you prepare:

1. Overall Message - What do I want my audience to take away from my message?
2. Outline - What is the general outline for my presentation that supports this overall message? What main points do I want to make?

3. Outcomes - What do I want my audience to think, feel or do as a result of what they will learn from me? How do I want their lives to be different?

The overall take-away message comes first and then the points extracted from that, not vice versa. Preparation and careful positioning of the content and elements you use to emphasize your points, also frees up mental clutter to allow you to connect more authentically with your audience.

Whether you use visuals, graphs, or Y*outube* clips within your presentations, each should be related to your points and be strategically positioned in the overall flow of your message. If you try to link the points without having an overall understanding of how they relate to each other and to the ultimate message then you compromise cohesiveness.

Look at one of your messages and see how you have positioned the points.

Do they align with the overall message? Is there a natural flow from one to the other?

Application:

How can you better prepare so that when you present you are able to freely engage with the audience? For more detailed instructions on how to be better prepared, pick up a copy of my best-selling book *Preparing to Speak: 8 Things You Need to Know Before You Step Onto the Platform.*

Content

17.

◦∞◦

Leverage Personal Experiences

Patricia Fripp, well-sought after Speaker and Speaking Coach says that "the secret to developing good content is simply this: you have to live an interesting life and converse with interesting people." When I first heard her say that, I asked myself, "what about if you haven't lived an interesting life nor conversed with interesting people? Can you still develop good content?"

If you were wondering the same thing, the answer is "yes, you can!"

One of the beautiful aspects of becoming a speaker who goes beyond communicating to connecting with your audience is that your personal experiences are valuable content. No matter what your history or type of presentation there are stories, events and experiences in your personal and professional life that will be valuable to include as content.

Where you can get stuck is if you start to minimize your experiences as irrelevant or not interesting. I want to caution you to stop! Don't do that! You will be amazed at how even one sentence from your past can have huge impact in a presentation when appropriately inserted.

Fripp suggests a process to follow when you analyze and organize your experiences. I encourage you to keep a file with the following information and lists:

- All the people who have influenced you in your life.
- Every manager or boss you've ever worked for.
- Write down what you have learned from each of them. (Even if they weren't nice)
- How do these lessons play out in your life up until today?
- List all the turning points in your life, who you met, and significant moments.
- What is some of the best advice you have been given?

That should trigger a flow of ideas about how to powerfully leverage your experiences to connect with your audience and create presentations and messages that are remembered and relevant.

Application:

Create a File on your computer and start adding the above lists of information as a resource for future messages

18.

❧

Use Less Content For More Impact

Have you ever walked away from a presentation feeling overloaded with information and not knowing what to do with what you heard, if anything? This happens far too often because most speakers make the mistake of trying to cram as much information as possible into their speech. They forget that the message is not about them, nor about how much knowledge they can transfer in a short period of time. As you learned in an earlier chapter, the message is not about you (the speaker) but about "you" (the audience), and what the audience walks away with.

Here's a rule to help you avoid making this mistake. It is called the 10-1 Rule. This Rule goes like this:

For every 10 minutes of speaking you need to aim to communicate no more than 1 point.

So if you are giving a 60 minute keynote speech then you need to prepare 5 points or less to include in your speech. That means that for every point you want to make you need to include ways to hit home the point in order to reinforce the learning.

Audiences become overwhelmed when speakers try to get across too much information in too little time. Overwhelm can paralyze people and leave them confused or uncertain as to how to apply what they heard. Even worse, audiences tune out when there is too much information coming at them. I learned this the hard way. When I first started out as a speaker, I was invited to give a 60 minute message only to find out when I arrived that my time was cut in half due to another speaker going overtime. I did what most people would have done, especially if you are a new speaker, I stood up, looked at my notes and spoke as fast as I could to get out as much information as possible until my time was up. Even though I did manage to get out all the information I had prepared to say, I had lost my audience a long time ago. That became a turning point in my life as I realized that day that speaking is not so much about giving information, but more about evoking transformation in the hearts and minds of the listeners. I understand that this is a skill that needs to be developed and requires a shift in the speaker's mindset about the purpose of their message. Implementing the 10-1 Rule will help you form the necessary speaking habits to leave a greater impact.

So if you are asked to speak for 35 minutes how many points can you make? I bet you said 3 and a half points, didn't you? Most speakers find themselves tempted to do the same: trying to squeeze in as much as possible. It is much better to round down and include only 3 points (or even better - two).

Remember this important Speaker proverb:

"When you squeeze your information in, you squeeze your audience out."

If you have more information on a topic than you can deliver in a given message, that would be a great reason for them to hire you for a longer event. Believe me, if you stick to this 10-1 Rule your chances of being re-hired will be greatly increased.

Application:

Review a message you have previously given or are working on. Apply the 10-1 Rule and determine how many points will fit within the time frame you are given. Re-write the message using the 10-1 Rule.

19.

⚮

Use the Power of Three

Do you know what number is the most important in creating your message? It's the number 3!

Using the **Rule of 3** will help make your speech or message clearer, more enjoyable and more memorable. The human brain can only process and retain so much information in a given period of time.

To keep your audience engaged, it is important to let them know how they can benefit from listening to you and your message. So it is helpful to let them know how many keys or points you are going to present so they know what to expect, and can stay engaged.

Transformational speakers have found that the way you package your points will affect how memorable your speech will be. For some unknown reason, giving information in chunks of three is most effective. So if you have more than three points to give, divide the information into chunks of three.

Instead of saying "you will receive nine keys to…" break the nine keys into three sections of three. If you are offering a full day workshop and have 27 points, break the information into three sections. Try it and watch what happens!

Application:

How can you divide your content into chunks of 3?

20.

‿‿∞‿‿

Make it Repeatable

One of the keys that make a top-notch speaker, is intentionally using tools to make your message memorable long after you finish speaking. Transformational speakers desire to impact people's lives not just when they are in front of them, but months and even years after they hear you speak. One powerful tool that will help you accomplish this is called a **Repeatable Phrase**. This phrase forms the foundation of your message or point and it is also repeatable and easy to remember. It helps the message stick with the audience longer.

This tool was first introduced to me as a "foundational phrase." As I applied it over the years, I adapted the concept for my coaching clients and re-named it.

The *Repeatable Phrase* is critical when creating a speech because it serves several purposes. First of all, it serves as the foundation or grid for you to determine what gets included in your presentation and what gets left out.

Just remember: "*The phrase determines what stays.*" (Oh, by the way, this is an example of a Repeatable Phrase).

Secondly, having a Repeatable Phrase helps bring clarity and focus to the overall message or individual points. The most effective Repeatable Phrases are 10 words or less. By keeping it short and crisp, it forces you to gain greater clarity about what you want your audience to take away. This phrase is also repeated at appropriate times in your message to help make it stick and to reinforce the learning of the points you are making. Although it does not need to rhyme, having a rhythmic sound to it increases the chance of it being remembered. For example, a repeatable phrase I use in one of my messages goes like this: "Don't just go through life, grow through it."

If you are not clear about your point, your audience won't be either. Having a strong Repeatable Phrase helps make your message clear, succinct, and memorable. Isn't that the kind of impact you want to leave with your audience? It also helps you as a speaker remember the points you are trying to make so you don't have to memorize your message word for word.

Start using Repeatable Phrases, and see how much more of your message audience members will remember long after you finish speaking!

Application:

How can you summarize your message (or one of your points) in ten words or less?

21.

❦

Don't Retell a Story, Relive It

One of the distinguishing factors between average speakers and Transformational Speakers is how they relay stories. You don't have to be a drama major or even dramatic to be a great story-teller. There are techniques, however, that when implemented will enhance your message to make it more memorable and transformational.

The first key is in understanding the difference between narration and storytelling. Instead of re-telling stories, my mentor Craig Valentine suggests you find ways to invite your audience into your "re-living" room. Storytelling is more about re-living rather than re-telling an incident. When you invite your audience to relive the story with you, you are painting a picture for them to imagine and to step into the scenes with you. Images stick with people longer than just words.

Narrating or re-telling always puts your message in the past. When you invite your audience to relive it, then it's as if they are right there beside you experiencing it with you, in the present, as it unfolds. It's the difference between watching a sports game from the stands versus being on the field and in the middle of the action, play by play.

As you plan where to put your story in your message, ask yourself "where in my scene do I want my audience members to be?". Then you can invite them into the story using statements such as "Imagine you had been sitting in the passenger seat that day as we drove through the darkened tunnel…". Or "If you had been standing next to me that day when we heard the news… you would have seen …".

To help your audience relive your story, find ways to include them in your scene. Remember, "experience is a better teacher." It may take some fine-tuning but inviting your audience into your experience will make your message that much more memorable. It will be as if they experienced it, therefore your point will stick in their minds longer and have a much more lasting impact.

Application:

Seek out a coach to help you fine-tune the skill of storytelling so you can re-live your stories instead of simply re-telling them."

22.

$\sim\!\!\infty\!\!\sim$

Give Your Point a Story

Stories are one of the most effective tools to illustrate a point. The primary purpose of a story is to have your audience experience your point and therefore accept it on their own without you having to convince them to. Let the story do the persuading.

Stories consist of 3 primary sections:

1. Setting the scene- establish the setting, time, characters, and conflict.
2. How the characters attempt to solve their problem or resolve their conflict, but with no success.
3. Resolution of the conflict by a hero. It's important to **not** make yourself the hero.

Before you begin, be clear on what your relationship is to the story and the characters in the story. For example, are you an onlooker telling from an observer's viewpoint, or are you in the story as one of the characters? In delivering your story, be original, develop your own style and connect your story to a point you are making. Let the story do the work it is designed for- to help the audience experience and accept the point without you having to convince them.

Application:

What stories can you use to illustrate your main points in a message? How can you construct it in such a way that draws your listeners in?

23.

Hook Your Audience Early

You have probably heard it said that the greatest speakers are storytellers and there is definitely some truth to that! However, it is not just telling a story that makes you an effective speaker it's *how* you present the story and use it to make a personal *connection* with your audience.

During my World Class Coach training, I learned about a method of storytelling that includes the "9 C's Formula." You can learn more about each of these C's in my **Emerging Women Speakers Academy!** For today, let's discuss the "C" that will keep your audience on the edge of their seats.

One of my coaches, Craig Valentine, is a master storyteller and several years ago, he reminded me that the *hook* for any speech is a story. Well-presented stories capture the audience's attention quicker than simple information. And the hook for any story is the struggle, or the *conflict*. The conflict, therefore, is the primary hook for your speech.

Identify the conflict in a story you want to include in a message. If your audience can relate to the specific conflict, they will buy into the solution, or the "cure" that you present.

This is why using a story is such an effective tool as an opener and as a means to connecting with your audience. A key to remember when conveying a story is "don't tell, show."

As you begin your story, set the stage by introducing the characters and inviting the audience into the scene. This is part of *re-living the story*. Immediately after you introduce your characters you need to throw them into the conflict, or problem, or dilemma they are facing.

Don't make the mistake that most speakers make and take too long in setting the scene and wait too long before creating the conflict. You will lose your audience if you don't create the conflict early on. But that's not all! The best speakers take it one step further and *escalate* the conflict. This is what is commonly done in movies to keep the audience intrigued and curious to keep watching. Let's take the famous movie *The Titanic*, for example. The conflict was created when the ship hit the iceberg, and then escalated as the water came into the boat and started slowly filling up over time, intensifying the conflict.

As a speaker you need to get the conflict to a point where something has to give and a decision has to be made. This is critical if you are presenting a service, a product or a solution to a problem. Remember, if your audience can't relate to the conflict they won't buy into the cure.

Whether you are sharing a testimonial, doing a presentation, or giving a motivational speech, be sure to incorporate some kind of conflict that the audience can relate to. In doing so, you will find it easier to keep your audience engaged and wanting more.

Application:

Think of story that you want to use in a message to illustrate a point. Identify the conflict in the story. How does that conflict become even more intense? Write out how you can structure the story so you introduce the conflict early and then plan how you will escalate it.

24.

∽

Pump Life into Your Message

In the last tip you learned that the *hook* to any story is the conflict and in this tip you'll discover that the *heart* of any story is dialogue!

If you want your message to go from boring to stimulating, avoid the use of narration and add dialogue when sharing a story. Dialogue acts like the heart does to the human body and pumps life into the story. It helps to bring the audience into the reality of the scene to relive the story with you. Narration acts like a report, whereas dialogue brings life to the story. Here are some of the effects of using dialogue when storytelling.

Dialogue helps your audience imagine your characters better because they can hear exactly how your character said something.

It allows you to display vocal variety, and expressions that are hidden in strictly narration.

It enables you to connect with the listeners at deeper levels because of them re-living the story with you.

It helps create a picture in the mind of the listener, that stays in the memory longer than words. Renown speaker and speaking coach, Patricia Fripp once said, "People remember more of what they *see* when they hear you speak than the words you say."

Using dialogue provides more opportunity to uncover humor.

Another World Champion Speaker (2001), Darren LaCroix, says that "Reactions tell the story." Using dialogue sets up wonderful opportunities for one character to react to another.

Here's the difference: Dialogue goes like this – "The young girl said, 'You've got to be kidding! I actually won?'"

Whereas narration would say – "The young girl couldn't believe that she won and thought the announcer was playing a joke on her." Can you *feel* the difference?

Application:

So the next time you need to breathe a little life into your story, use dialogue! And then use even more dialogue!

25.

⤡

It's What You Take Out of a Message That Makes the Difference

One of the biggest mistakes people make when creating a keynote message or speech is trying to say too much in the time allotted! When you lay out the contents of your message one of the first things you need to do is answer this question: *What do you want your audience to think, feel and do as a result of experiencing you?*

Knowing the answer to this question will help you determine what information, stories and details to include in your message. More importantly, it will help you determine what not to include! You may be struggling in this area because some of the content is personal and sacred to you. Not including it in this message does not mean it will be lost but simply that it will be better used in another message.

Often when speakers share stories they include lots of details that are extraneous or not necessary to the point. This can potentially have a negative impact if it causes the story to drag on and distract the listeners from staying engaged. Details included in a story should serve to support and emphasize the point and all others should be left out. Creating compelling content is a creative process and often the overall impact of the message is determined by what you are willing to take out rather than by what you put in. Get a vision for what you want the message to look like and follow Michelangelo's approach to creating a masterpiece.

Michelangelo said of his sculpture;

"I saw the angel in the marble and I carved until I set him free."

Application:

Hold your stories and content with an open hand and take the time to reflect on whether each piece is adding to, or taking away from the points you are wanting to make. Knowing your purpose, and the answer to the above question is a great filter to help you in that process and will guide you in what needs to be removed so your masterpiece emerges.

26.

∾

Turn Your Content Into a Keynote

What is a Keynote message?

A seminar or workshop is meant to help people develop skill sets, whereas a Keynote is often used for helping audiences get in the right mindset.

Depending on whether you are doing the opening or closing keynote your objectives will be different. Usually an opening keynote is more about inspiring people than teaching people tools. One of the biggest mistakes speakers make is trying to give too much information in the time they have to speak. This is where applying the 10-1 Rule is very important. A keynote message is different from a signature message in both purpose and length. The typical length of a keynote message is around sixty to ninety minutes. Therefore, you need to learn the skill of not just adding more content but keeping your audience engaged and interested in listening to you for a longer period of time.

Does writing a keynote message come easy to you? Most people labour for days trying to put together a message, not even sure where to begin. If that's true for you think of *developing* a speech rather than *writing* one.

The three main sections in a keynote message are:

1. The Opening
2. The Main Points or The Body
3. The Closing

Don't make the mistake that most speakers make and start writing your keynote from the beginning, the very first words you want to open with and continue to the closing words. However, your message needs to be developed in a different order than what you speak. For example, your opening should be a *preview* of your main points, therefore you need to know what your main points are before you write your opening. The closing is to include a *review* of your main points and often circle back to how you opened. So the first thing you need to decide on is: What main points do you want your audience to take away?

Here's the process I follow when I am creating a new message:

1. Take time to quiet yourself and meditate on the topic or overall message you want to leave with the audience. Quieting yourself may mean going to a coffee shop, sitting in nature, taking a prayerful posture, or going for a walk. Writing your thoughts on a whiteboard or large wall size post-it note is a great way to brainstorm. I often ponder ideas or points over a few days before writing anything down. Then I go to my white board and list the main points I want to include in that message.
2. Ask yourself, "What do I want the audience to think/feel or do after hearing my message?" (Yes I know, I keep

repeating this. I hoping you get the point that it is a very important question to answer).

3. Determine the 3-5 main points you want to leave with your audience.

4. Then I answer the question: "What's the exact next step I want my audience to take after I finish speaking? "The answer to this question becomes part of your closing.

I encourage you to try following a similar process the next time you need to create a new message. And when you do, I believe you will gain far greater clarity about what you want to say and experience increased confidence when it comes time to speak.

Application:

Determine the purpose of your keynote message and list the top three points you want to include to accomplish that purpose.

Aim for Connection Not Perfection

27.

༄

Go The Extra Mile With A Simple Smile

Several years ago I worked as a Speech-Language Pathologist. I started my career working with children who were delayed in their speech and language development and then I opened my own practice specializing in accent reduction with adults. Early on in my university degree training I was taught that 93% of what a person communicates is actually non-verbal. That means only 7% of what you communicate is conveyed through your words alone.

In the next few tips you will learn about some of the communication keys that make up that nonverbal area. These all come into play in the delivery process of your message or speech. Even if the percentages were much less such as 75%, tell yourself that you will connect much deeper and longer with your audience if you focus your energy on developing the habits that impact your nonverbal communication.

The first habit you need to develop in order to build trust and credibility with your audience is to smile often (and appropriately). Remember the audience is usually most skeptical about the speaker at the beginning of the presentation or message. As a speaker, that is usually the time you are most nervous. If not properly planned, your opening can soon become a disaster.

The simplest thing you can do to exude confidence, which will also help your audience gain confidence in you, is to simply smile. Before you even say a word- smile warmly while looking at the audience. Think of it as your introduction to your audience. When you first meet someone you usually smile and shake their hand or give them a hug. This has the same effect.

It is of course understood that when you smile, it needs to be genuine and not forced. Otherwise it will communicate a different message. Throughout your presentation remember to smile at other appropriate times to continue to connect with your audience and build trust and credibility.

A simple smile will bridge your connection, build a warm atmosphere, and boost the audience's confidence in you.

If it helps you, here is a saying I came up with to remind me:

"A simple smile can take you the extra mile".........towards building trust and credibility.

Application:

Smile more when you speak.

28.

❧

Connect With Your Audience Before You Speak

Did you know that how you show up *before* you speak *also* plays a role in helping you connect with your audience at the time you start to speak?

The most sought after speakers arrive early to a speaking appointment in order to take time to personally interact and greet the members of the audience that day. This demonstrates a well known principle in establishing trust: *"familiarity helps breed confidence."* By interacting with individuals personally, even briefly, you help to break down any awkwardness of coming into a new group and makes the audience more open to trust you.

If you find yourself still working through lots of nervousness when you speak, then doing this may especially help you. Take time prior to taking the stage, to get to know 2-3 friendly people in the audience. Then once you get up to speak, start out by looking at these friendly, and now familiar, faces to help settle your nervousness.

You may even make reference to a comment during the conversation with one of them if appropriate or relevant. For example, you may say "when I came this morning, I met Lori and I was intrigued by how she achieved her goal of … this is a great example of one of the keys you're going to learn about today in the area of … "

Try this next time and notice the difference it makes.

If you show up and stick to yourself and don't take time to connect with others personally you will hinder the process of building trust before you even open your mouth.

How you conduct yourself "offstage" is just as important as how you conduct yourself "onstage!" Who you are "off camera" needs to be consistent with who you are "on camera" if you want your audience to even begin to like and trust you.

Application:

Show up early to a speaking engagement and connect with some of the audience members.

29.

❦

Build Trust Through Eye Contact

Have you ever been in a conversation with someone and they couldn't maintain eye contact for five seconds? Did they look down or away from you as they spoke? What went on inside of you when that happened? What did you feel or think?

The worst is when you are in a conversation and the person speaking keeps looking over your shoulder at someone else in the room making gestures to them or giving them more eye contact than you. If you are like me, I feel like getting up a walking away in that moment.

Sadly, I have been one of those people who looked over my listener's shoulder and became sorely aware of how offensive and insensitive that can be.

Eye contact is the most underemphasized part of communication yet it is one of the most crucial areas that help you establish trust and credibility with your listeners. Making appropriate eye contact with your listeners is absolutely essential as a speaker to deliver a convincing message. Frequent and intentional eye content is your ongoing link with your audience. In the next section you will learn a tip on the powerful use of eye contact.

30.

∽

Look To All,
Speak To One

R ecently, I was listening to a speaker deliver a great message. The content was very practical and the message very clear. However, throughout the speech I felt somewhat disconnected. I kept wanting him to look up more. I wanted to see his eyes. For the majority of the 60 minutes, he spoke with his eyes glued on his notes.

Unfortunately, this scenario is very typical among speakers, especially if you are focused on getting it "right", giving a perfect presentation. In another tip, you learned that the most important word as a speaker is the word "you." This week you will learn how to take the power of that word one step further.

What is important to realize is that your job as a speaker is not simply to *give information* but also to *evoke transformation*. Even though you tailor your sentences so that you are using the singular word "you" when addressing the audience, you also need to be mindful that maintaining regular eye contact will serve to deepen the connection even further.

Remember that over 90% of communication is nonverbal. That means, that the words you say are only a small fraction of what *sticks with* your audience, long after you finish speaking.

For many years I worked as a Speech Language Pathologist, and started a side business providing Accent Reduction Coaching. Much of what makes up an accent is found in the way vowels are pronounced, and in the intonation that accompanies the words. In addition to the intonation, tone and variety in the voice, what you do with your body, as a public speaker, is a critical piece in effectively connecting with your audience. You will learn more about delivery tips later. For now, let's focus on the eyes.

To stand out as a speaker, begin to practice this simple rule: *Look to all, speak to one*!

That means that if you want to increase your effectiveness as a speaker, practice maintaining significant amount of eye contact by naturally scanning the audience looking at the people regularly throughout your message. As you do, you will find yourself able to keep your audience more engaged. There will be times when it will be more effective to briefly focus on one person with your eyes for emphasis. For example, You may say "What would *you* do if you only had 30 secs to make *that* decision?" and briefly pause while looking in the eyes of one audience member and then scanning the room as the whole audience reflects on what they would do.

Most speakers stay glued to their notes because they are more concerned with getting out all the information rather than being a catalyst for transformation.

If you want to stand out as a speaker with impact, go one step further in your preparations: *don't just memorize your message, internalize it*! Remind yourself that the message is about your audience and what they walk away with, not about you and what you have to give. Taking time to prepare and internalize your message will help give you freedom to focus more on connecting with your audience using eye contact and purposeful movement.

Application:

Next time you give a presentation deliberately use your eyes to deepen the connection with a specific audience and observe what difference it makes.

31.

 ∞

Use You-Focused Language

A mong the most basic needs that human beings have is the need to connect with another human being intellectually, spiritually, emotionally and physically. Communication is the word we use to describe the process of making and keeping this connection. Most women speakers become anxious and nervous because they are focused on giving a perfect presentation and worry that they will forget some of the words they prepared to say. If you are focused on perfectionism, you miss out on the most important job of a speaker: making a personal connection with your audience.

There are several tools that successful speakers use to connect with their audience. Today's tip is about how you can structure your language to make that connection, and specifically, about the use of "You-focused" sentence structures. Have you ever started a presentation something like this?

"Today I'm going to share with you some tools….," or "Today I am going to teach you how to.." We all have. But the reality is that the audience doesn't care what you want to do, or how much you know. It's true they don't. All they care about is what they are going to receive or how they are going to benefit from what you have to say. With this fact in mind, whenever you find yourself saying something like: "today I am going to teach you…," ask yourself how you can reword the structure to make it more audience focused. Instead you can say something like this: "today *you* will pick up 5 keys…," or "in the next 30 minutes *you* are going to receive…." *"You"* is the most important word in speaking and more importantly in connecting with your audience. *It's never about what the speaker gives, it's always about what you get.* *"You"*, in this sentence, refers to the audience. That is why *"you"* is the most important word in speaking. It's human nature for audience members to be subconsciously asking, "what's in it for me?" As a speaker, you need to keep this in mind when structuring your presentation and speeches. It is essential that you don't wait until the end to answer that question for the audience but intersperse bits of the answer throughout your speech. This will keep your audience engaged and wanting to hear more.

It's important here to make the distinction between a *hard you* and a *soft you*. Old traditional styles of preaching often included the use of *hard you* type of sentences. To help you understand the difference, think about how it makes you feel when a speaker says the following: "You need to stop complaining about your spouse and be more thankful." Compared to: "What impact will it have on your relationship if you focused more on what you are thankful for about that person?" Can you *feel* the difference in the way an audience responds internally to each of those sentences? The first one makes the audience feel like they are being told what to do, whereas, the second one is inviting them to consider how their life would be different if they changed their focus.

Application:

As you write your next speech or tweak an existing one, consider what question you can ask in order to get your audience to think about their own situation. Plan the question into your message and see what happens with the level of audience engagement you receive. If you want to become a transformational speaker, remember to *focus on connection, not perfection.*

32.

Keep Them On the Edge of Their Seats

Transformational speakers also do *You-focused check-ins* throughout their speech to not only connect with their audience but to *maintain* the connection. Here's a few examples of how to use *you-focused check-ins:* "Raise *your* hand if *you* have ever overreacted in a situation." (gets audience to reflect on how it relates to them). "What would you have done if that was your daughter lying on that field?" "If *you* had seen me 5 years ago *you* would have noticed that I was 40 pounds heavier than I am today." These statements *invite* the audience to step into whatever story or point you are making and allow you to connect with them at a personal level. The key to doing *you-focused* check-ins is to search for similarities and give opportunities for your audience members to personally reflect on something. Ask yourself, "what do I have in common with the people in this particular audience?" Whatever you have in common, make the check-in about that. This not only keeps your audience engaged in your story, but it reminds them that the message is about them (not about what you want to teach them).

As well, make the "you" singular and not plural so you get a more personal response. For example, most speakers use this kind of sentence structure: "How many of you...?" which is a plural "you" and therefore gives a group response (non-personal). Instead, use the singular "you" and say it like this: "Have you ever...?" "Do you...?" which enables you to make a more personal connection. If you want to stand out as woman speaker, pay attention to your choice of words and sentence structure, and intentionally plan into your message opportunities to connect with your listeners using "you-focused" language.

Application:

When preparing your message, make sure you structure the sentences so your use of "you" is singular, not plural. Plan in regular check-ins with the audience to keep them engaged and reflecting.

33.

〜∞〜

Don't Memorize, Internalize

Whenever I hear and watch a speaker who is constantly looking at their notes I can't help but wonder what's going on for them. Are they nervous? Are they unprepared? Or both? Whatever the reason, what goes on inside the listeners is more important. As an aspiring or experienced speaker, if you are struggling with being glued to your notes, I want to challenge you to do whatever it takes to get comfortable with looking up.

Getting comfortable looking out into the audience starts with dealing with embracing personal transformation as you deal with your own stuff! When I first became aware of my discomfort, I realized that it was because I was insecure and did not want people to discover that. You have probably heard the saying "The eyes are windows into the soul." Pursuing personal growth and development is key to growing in confidence as a communicator. Who you are on the inside will shine through whether you want it to or not. One way it's revealed is in how you engage with people. Once I opened myself up to be coached in this area I experienced tremendous freedom in my interactions with people both one on one and in large groups.

When is it okay to look at your notes? A rule of thumb in the speaking world is to make eye contact at the beginning and end of a sentence. The best and most effective time to look at your notes is in the middle of a sentence. This will take some practice but very quickly it will become second nature to you. What does that mean? Your preparation is vital. To be a more effective speaker you will need to develop the discipline of really knowing your speech or message.

But *don't memorize it, internalize it.*

This will free your mind to focus on engaging your audience at various points throughout your presentation and help your message flow more naturally.

Application:

Learn to internalize your messages so you are free to connect with your audiences.

34.

❧

Be Known As Similar, Not Special

Not long ago I heard a woman speaker who had gained great success over the years. Her message was that she went from rags to riches and told just how she did it. Although she was giving the process and conveying how she did it I was left feeling uninspired by what she had to say. As a result I had no desire to look further into her programs or resources. As I reflected on why, I realized that how she communicated her journey made her appear "special", and therefore did not leave me with the sense that if she can do it, then so can I. Even though I knew in my head I could. My response was purely an emotional one but one that is key in connecting with any audience.

As a speaker *"when you lift yourself up, you let your audience down."*

Unless you come across as "similar" to your audience they will not connect with your message nor be motivated to act on any steps you give or anything you offer as a resource. It's critical that you tell your story and the journey that took you from where you were to where you are today. However, in doing so, it's important to point out where you are no different than those in your audience, and how the things that helped you can help them. In order to connect with your audience you need to be relevant and relatable. If you desire to have a greater impact when you speak, become known as "similar and not special".

Application:

What can you include in your message to help your audience see you as similar to them?

35.

❧

Put First Things First

Whether you are speaking on a tele-seminar or on a stage, you have already learned that establishing trust and credibility is absolutely essential. If your audience is familiar with you and consists of regular clients then you can modify your opening to suit that context. Say you have been invited as a guest on a tele-seminar to give your signature talk to a new audience. In addition to opening with a *bang*, it is important to spend the first few minutes of your 60 minute talk building trust with your audience. This can be accomplished in two primary ways:

1. **Credibility:** Include enough background information about yourself to help the audience become familiar with you and your expertise in the topic. This is best done when the host introduces you. Write your own introduction so the host gives the accolades, and not you. Then as you start your talk you can establish more credibility by sharing stories or testimonials of previous clients.

2. **Vulnerability:** Another way to help your audience become familiar with you and trust you is to share some area of frailty or flaw you had to overcome. This helps the audience feel like you can relate to where they are at. For example, you may be speaking about a four part

process you use to help young girls overcome an eating disorder and establish a healthy lifestyle. As part of your opener, include the fact that you also struggled with an eating disorder years ago. And after trying everything else to get better that you stumbled upon this process which finally gave you what you needed to break the cycles and become healthy. This bridges the gap between them seeing you simply as a so-called expert and them trusting that you understand their daily struggles.

Building trust in these two ways helps you make a better connection with your audience from the start, and increases the likelihood of them staying engaged throughout the rest of your talk.

Application:

What can you include in your message to help your audience naturally build trust and credibility in you?

36.

∽

Share Your Accolades Authentically

Many speakers struggle with how much of their background they should share before it starts sounding boastful. It is important to share some of your accolades to build credibility. The key is how you share it that makes the difference. As the audience members listen they will be asking themselves, "Why should I be listening to this person?" or "How did this person get the right to speak on that topic?"

Somewhere in your message you want to help answer those questions. Here are some suggestions on how to do that effectively but gracefully.

1) Spread it throughout your message. Instead of giving your complete background and credentials at the front, spread it throughout your message as is appropriate to different points you make. eg. "This next tool is one I picked up when I worked as the National Sales Manager with..."

2) Share one or two failures before you share accolades. This not only helps build credibility and trust but doesn't make it come across as boasting when you do share your accolades.

3) Put the process on the pedestal before the person. When talking about wins, put it in the context of processes that helped you make that win to avoid putting yourself on the pedestal. eg. "I found myself surrounded by extremely creative people and it was their constant influence that helped stimulate my own innovation and contributed to my success."

4) Share your accolades through others. This is where testimonials can play a huge role. Whether it is part of a story you share or a live testimonial, both are excellent ways to let the audience know why they should trust in what you are saying.

Application:

Try these four ways to sharing your background and observe the difference it makes in how others perceive and receive you.

37.

⚈⚈⚈

Think Like Your Audience

ttention spans are getting shorter especially for audio presentations. As speakers you will have to be more creative in how you deliver messages if you want to engage your audience and make your message stick.

One way to increase your ability to engage is to learn to think like your audience members. As you prepare the content of your message, say it out loud and reflect on how your words may potentially trigger a question or objection in the minds of your listeners. Then address those questions and objections in your message. Include your responses in your content. You can bring them out into the open by saying something like "Some of you are already formulating arguments in your mind as you why you couldn't do that." Or "a question you may be asking yourself is.....", "Let's take a minute to briefly discuss that objection."

Learning to put yourself in your listener's shoes will serve to make a deeper connection with them and keep them engaged throughout your message. Give it a try!

Application:

How can you demonstrate that you are thinking like your audience the next time you give a talk?

38.

◦◦◦

Be Aware of the Silent Killers

It is a known fact that good communication is the foundation of successful relationships, both personally and professionally. But as you have learned, your communication involves much more than words. Studies show that at least 55% of communication is nonverbal and even higher (93%) if you include tone of voice, facial expressions, and body language.

The reality is that your nonverbal communication will always say more than your words. It is the silent language that speaks louder than your verbal. Even when you stop speaking you are still sending messages and communicating non-verbally. In his book, "The Art of Non-Verbal Selling" author Gerhard Gschwandtner states that even during an average 30 minute sales call (by phone) you are exchanging approximately 800 non-verbal messages. Imagine what that means when you are face-to-face or in front of an audience. How many nonverbal messages are you sending when in person?

As a speaker, it is important then to become more in tune with your body language and other non-verbal cues. This will also result in you becoming more in tune with your thoughts and feelings. As you do, you become aware of the signals you are communicating to your listeners and if needed make the necessary adjustments to make sure your non-verbal communication is congruent, lines up, with what you really want to communicate.

Today I want to emphasize a simple concept to help you maintain an open posture when you are speaking in front of people.

Make an intention to always keep an open body posture. This means be aware of your arms and legs when sitting to make sure they are not crossed when sitting down in conversation. When standing and speaking remember that if you stand behind a table or podium you are blocking your audience from connecting with you. If possible, move away from a lectern or podium as much as possible to keep the lines of connection open. Anything that gets between you and your listeners, including a laptop or projector stand, will affect your ability to connect as deeply as you should.

This is a new shift in modern communication and important to note. Historically, it was more acceptable to stand behind a podium for your whole message or speech. This style feels less personal to this era of audiences. Today, authentic communication is expected and invites more collaboration and connection.

Application:

This week, observe your body language as you converse with others. Does it match what you want to communicate? If not, what do you need to adjust so your posture and stance aligns with what you really want to say?

39.

∽✕∾

Reflection Leads To Deeper Connection

Speakers often measure their success on whether or not their audience stayed and listened to them. If no one walked out and everyone paid attention then you may think you are doing well. And you may be doing well by keeping your audience's attention, but how well did you do at making a connection? Keep in mind that to be most effective as a communicator you need to learn ways to move your audience to action. It is not enough to have your audience listen to you, your goal is to get them to listen to themselves. One way you can do this is by getting them to reflect. Getting your listeners to think about how they will apply your message increases the odds of them actually applying it to their life long after your message is over. It is not enough to have them reflect on the content for the purpose of remembering and regurgitating it, you need to invite them to reflect on how the tips, tools or solutions you are offering will benefit their life.

Here is a 3-Step formula to getting your audience to reflect. I call it my *Reflection APP:*

1. **A-**Ask them open-ended questions throughout your message.

2. **P**-Pick something out of your story (a word, a concept, etc) for them to apply.
3. **P**-Put it in your audience's life by using the same word in a specific open-ended question.

For example, in one of my messages I talk about a story in which I needed to "get through the mess to get to the message". I then ask the audience. "What mess in your life have you been avoiding?" By using the same word used in my story, "the mess" I had them put it in their own life and reflect on how my solution may apply to them.

It is important to also use lots of open-ended questions throughout your entire speech or message. Be sure to place them strategically to get your audience continually reflecting. But it is equally important to use the *Reflection APP* above to have them intentionally reflect about how your message can apply to their life.

When you are creating your next speech, what can you take out of your story, put it into the audience's life and have them reflect on?

As Craig Valentine says, *"When you make your audience reflect, you have the greatest effect!"*

Keep in mind that to have a transformational impact you need to learn to deepen the personal connection with your audience. *Reflection helps make that personal connection.*

Application:

Implement the APP formula to make a deeper connection with your audience.

Closing with Impact

40.

❧

Use Only One Exact Next Step

People remember best what they hear first and last. One common mistake among speakers is having a weak ending to their presentation or message. Many speakers simply let the closing part of their speech "just happen" which results in leaving the audience just hanging or disengaged.

If you want to become a more effective communicator it is imperative that you spend time preparing how you will close your message. All that you said up to this part in the message is to bring the audience to some action or response. A strong closing will outline a clear call to action including a next step. You need to be clear on what you want your audience to do immediately after your message and how they can best implement what you have said.

This helps make your message more personal and more practical. Don't fall into the trap of thinking it is better to give a few options at the end of a message. Whether you are speaking to grow your business, raise funds, expand your influence or inspire people to take action, having *only one* exact next step is always better.

With the rapid development of technology you and I have more options available to us to choose from than any other time in history. You would think that this would cause us to make decisions quicker, but research shows just the opposite. People become paralyzed when they are offered too many options, even two. There is a fear of missing out or making the wrong choice that often results in no action being taken. When you intentionally focus on only one exact next step, the choice is much clearer and those who choose yes do so much quicker.

Why bother to include any call to action? That is the topic of another chapter.

Application:

Think about a message you are preparing or have given before. What exact next step can you invite your audience to take?

41.

Make Your Points Stick

Have you ever heard someone speak and their message was all over the place? When I was first started out as a public speaker, I was told that stories and jokes were good to tell to engage the audience. What I wasn't told was that the stories or jokes should be connected or anchored to a point.

What you are about to learn is a an incredible tool that makes your speech a raving success and gives your audience a message that sticks in their minds long after you finish speaking. Of all the tools I picked up from my coach training this is one of my favorites.

What's loose is lost. The most powerful tool is the use of Anchors. The goal of the Anchor is to make each of your points memorable. Anchors give you something to tie the point to so they don't get lost in people's mind. You do this by attaching each point to a story, activity, or something that will anchor to people's memory.

Psychologically, using anchors creates the power of association in people's minds.

Here are five of the most powerful types of anchors I use:

1) Acronym
2) Activity
3) Anecdote (ie. story)

4) Analogy

5) Audio-Visual

I have had the privilege of co-authoring a book with Craig and Mitch, and forty other speaking coaches, called *World Class Speaking In Action.* If you are interested in going deeper in your learning and developing the skills to become a transformational speaker, while connecting with other like-minded women who are doing the same, I highly recommend you check out www.emergingwomenspeakers.com which is my online training academy established exclusively for women who want to find their voice, and speak with confidence, clarity and impact.

Application:

Review a recent message you created and see where you can incorporate the use of an anchor to better illustrate your point.

42.

⌒∞⌒

Make Your Message Memorable

Have you ever listened to someone speak and an hour later forget what they said? Well, you are not alone. Studies suggest that the average person retains only a small amount of information they hear in a day. In particular, after one hour, most people retain less than 50% of what they heard. After one day, people are shown to forget more than 70% of what they were taught in a training session or workshop. One study suggested that forgetting is not all the learner's fault but how the information is presented can either hinder or solidify the memory. As a speaker, there are ways you can help your message become more memorable, so the impact on your audience lasts long after you stop speaking.

Well-known speaking coach, Patricia Fripp once said something like this: people won't remember exactly what you say as much as they will remember the images that came to mind when you were speaking.

Your job as a speaker is to help create the right images for them to remember.

Application:

What words and movements can you use to help create the images you want the audience to take away and remember long after you finish speaking?

43.

∽

A Shift in Perspective Can Make it More Effective

The famous motivational speaker Zig Ziglar once said that "even though you may be an excellent writer, you will not be an excellent oral communicator" if you approach the two the same way. By the way, the opposite is also true. You cannot approach speaking the same as writing otherwise you may come across as dull and hard to understand.

The best speakers know *that it's often one little shift in perspective that makes your speech that much more effective!*

Here are four differences between spoken and written language outlined by Ziglar in his book *Top Performance.*

When Speaking:

Language needs to be easily and instantly understood to the listener. Unlike written language, when the listener doesn't understand something you said he can't go back and re-read what you said.

Language should be more repetitive. Rephrasing and emphasizing key words through repetition are necessary for the listener to take away and remember your most important points.

Language needs to be simpler in structure than written language to enhance the listener's learning experience. Fewer words often has a bigger impact in speaking.

Use of figurative language can have a powerful impact on connecting deeply with your audience. However, it must be used strategically and appropriately for greatest affect.

Finally, one difference that I want to add is that spoken language is more conversational, whether you are speaking to an audience of one or one hundred. The listener needs to feel like you are speaking to them. At the same time, it requires more of your energy and your presence as you speak with passion and purpose.

Investing in improving your communication skills is a wise decision and will have huge payoffs in relationships, business growth and motivating others for positive change. Even though you first have to "write" your speech before you say it, you need to approach it from the perspective of the needs of the listener and how they hear it and write it as you want to say it.

Application:

What one little shift in perspective can you make that will help make your speech that much more effective?

44.

⸙

Last Impressions are Lasting Impressions

As mentioned before, most speakers completely neglect their closing and view it as unimportant. When in fact, how you close is extremely important and needs to be thoughtfully planned and done purposefully.

Last impressions are lasting impressions.

The last words that your audience is left thinking about will influence them the most. In planning your closing, keep in mind that it serves three main purposes:

1. *Recap* the learning. Review the points covered and any repeated phrases.

2. *Resolution* provided for any story you shared or a solution to a problem you addressed. This may include a closing story to inspire or motivate the audience as to the benefit of taking action.

3. *Respond* to a specific call to action. What do you want your listeners to do after hearing your presentation or message?

Application:

Take the time to plan your closing to make sure you are closing on purpose and are leaving your audience with the right impressions.

Captivating your Audience

45.

⌀

Boost Your Confidence Daily

As a public speaker, your level of confidence plays a huge role in how others perceive you and whether or not they see you as a credible authority in your field. Even at networking events, showing up with confidence can gain you instant credibility and open more doors of opportunity.

I first discovered the power of boosting your confidence on the spot from Dr. Cynthia Boccara, a chiropractor. She was talking on the power of presence. Of all the factors that make up your personal presence and help you present a good impression, how you carry yourself, your posture, has the most powerful impact on how others perceive you.

Scientists say that the simple act of adjusting your posture, can improve your energy levels, your relationships and even your income. In fact the research findings of Social Psychologist, Amy Cuddy, has shown that you can change people's perceptions of you and perhaps even your own body chemistry, simply by changing body positions. Her work at Harvard found that when people held this "POSTURE" position for 2 minutes, they experienced a 25% decrease in stress hormones and 50% increase in confidence or happy hormones.

To implement this, think back to when you were a child and would stand up against a wall or door frame so your parents could measure how much you had grown. This is similar except once you master it, you can do this whenever you find yourself lacking confidence whether you are sitting, standing or walking. The best way to learn it is in the form of the acronym developed by Boccara.

P- Pull up the crown of your head, without lifting your chin.

O- Orient your head over your shoulders, so it isn't tilted to one side. Think of your head like a bowling ball and hold it straight.

S-Shoulders. Lift your shoulders up, back and down so the joint is forward and you feel tension between your shoulder blades. However, be careful not to over-exaggerate this, as it will leave a different impression.

T- Tension. As you pull up on your head and back and down on your shoulders it creates a tension in your spine. This is really important because this tension is what triggers your brain to release a hormone that makes you feel more confident.

U- Untuck your pelvis. Think Beyonce booty. Again, don't over-exaggerate this either.

R- Roll back on your heels and align your hips over your ankles.

E- Exhale fully and lower the tone of your voice.

When you first do this it may seem like a lot to remember, just like when you first learned how to drive, however with practice it will soon become second nature and you will find yourself walking around with better posture.

This is one very simple, yet powerful way you can build confidence everyday in any situation you find yourself, whether sitting or standing.

Application:

The next time you have to speak and find yourself feeling a little anxious or uncertain, take 7 seconds, make the POSTURE adjustment, and experience the instant results in how you feel and exude more confidence.

(To have a visual instruction of this speaking tip, visit www.lisav.tv and look up the video with the same title as this tip.)

46.

Write Your Introduction

Whenever you are invited to speak somewhere make sure you provide the event organizer the words to use when introducing you. Send them a written introduction so they know exactly how you want to be introduced.

This helps to build credibility and trust with your audience even before you speak. In addition, many times the person who introduces you may not have had prior experience with you, and will not be able to vouch for your abilities. Also, depending on the demographics of your audience, you will want to tailor your introduction to emphasize parts of your bio that is more relevant to that audience and to the purpose for which they are coming to hear you.

By not planning your introduction and leaving it up to others you may find yourself being introduced in such a way that forces you to spend more time laying the groundwork of trust with the audience. Their expectation will be shaped by how you are introduced. If you are about to give a motivational speech and the person introducing you uses words to describe your business training and not your ability to motivate and inspire, then it may start the meeting off on a different tone. That part of your bio may be more relevant to a corporate audience and thus you may have to work harder at the front end to engage your audience.

When structuring your presentation or message, include the introduction as part of that structure. Even if you send it ahead in digital form always bring a hard copy with you in case the person introducing you forgets to bring it.

Application:

Think of an upcoming speaking opportunity and re-write your introduction, tailoring it to that exact audience and message objective.

47.

Capture Audience Attention From The Start

Did you know that in the first 7 seconds of your speech the audience will decide whether or not they like you? And in the first 30 seconds they will decide whether or not you are worth listening to? That means how you open your speech is absolutely key to establishing a connection with your audience. Most women speakers make the mistake of opening their message or speech with polite greetings or unpleasant pleasantries, such as "thank you so and so for inviting me here today. "Some may even start out by apologizing that they are not public speakers (even though they are speaking to a public audience when they say this). I have heard this and as an audience member it immediately lowers my expectation and makes me wonder why I should give up my time to listen. Transformational speakers know that you must catch the audience's attention right away and start off with a "wow" or an unexpected opening or a "bang." Contrary to what you may have been taught you should never open your speech with such statements as "I want to Thank....", "I am so excited to be here...", "How's everyone doing today?" or other clichés. Yes, I agree it is polite to acknowledge your host or thank them for the great introduction they gave you. I am not suggesting that you don't do that, just don't make it the *first* thing you say when you get to the podium. Instead, say it a few minutes into your speech and only after you have captured your audience's attention. This may take some practice but you will see a noticeable difference in how easily and effectively you engage your audience using this single tip.If you open your message like every other speaker, then you will be like every other speaker, and not stand out as different! By starting your message in an unexpected way, you immediately engage the audience and create a curiosity in them to want to hear more. With the increased use of technology in everyday life, this skill has become even more critical for speakers to learn how to engage their audiences right from the start and give listeners a reason to put down their mobile devices during the presentation. There are several ways you can open with a "Wow", however, two of the most effective ways are starting off with a *story* or asking a *powerful* (and relevant) *question*.

People remember best what they hear first and last! So if you start with a story, just jump right in telling your story and be sure to start at a place that immediately draws the audience in. Think of one of your favorite movies. How did the writer capture your attention from the opening scene? The storyline probably started in the middle of a scene then continued on by filling in the back story. Opening your message with a story allows you to powerfully connect with your audience, get them engaged at the first word, and leave them wanting to hear more. I will caution you here before you think that any story will do. Storytelling is an art and skill to be developed in an of itself. In a later chapter, you will learn more about some of the key components you need to include in order to make your story that much more captivating. For now, look at how you usually open your message and see how you can incorporate the use of a story.

Application:

What story can you use to open your message? How can you use it *capture* your audience's attention from the opening lines?

48.

◁∞▷

Create Curiosity

A
sking a question is another effective way to open your message. However, not any question will do. The most powerful questions elicit a response from the majority, if not all, the people in your audience. For example, in one of my training sessions on how to use speaking to grow your business and expand your influence as a leader, I start one of my messages with this question:

"Have you ever said something you wished you could take back?" Notice the difference if I had asked: "What's the biggest mistake you have ever made when speaking?"

The second question makes the audience wander in their mind in search of remembering a mistake they may have made at some time. However, the first question helps narrow the topic so the audience thinks immediately of a moment in time where they regretted something they said.

Capturing your audience's attention from the start is essential and takes careful planning. Therefore, knowing ahead of time what you are going to say as soon as you open your mouth is critical to engaging your audience. If you don't effectively capture their attention at the start, you may find yourself fighting to get it throughout the message. When using a question to open your message, make sure you pause briefly after you ask it. This gives your audience time to reflect on the answer and allows for a personal connection. Most speakers make the mistake of asking a question without giving *space* for the audience to answer the question in their mind and reflect on how it personally applies to them. Another common mistake is asking too many questions, stacking them one after the other. This often prevents the audience from stopping at one place in their mind as they try to process all the questions. The purpose of opening with a question should be to connect with your audience on a topic that relates to the rest of your message. That is why you need to carefully craft the question so it effectively engages your audience and helps them personally reflect. *Remember that when you get them to reflect, you have a greater effect.*

Application:

What question can you ask to get your audience engaged from the start?

49.

∞

How You Appear Can Draw Others Near

As you study the most effective speakers you will notice that they take great care in their appearance. I am not referring to having a perfectly matched outfit, perfect hair or sporting the newest fashion trend. I am referring to the fact that they understand that your appearance is part of your presentation. If you have a sloppy appearance or soiled clothing believe it or not, it may decrease the audience's ability to trust you. Now if you are speaking to a group of skateboarders then having baggy pants and ripped jeans may be what is needed to win their trust. Knowing your audience is important. You want to avoid wearing anything that may serve as a distraction to your audience. Let's talk about when speaking to a mixed audience. Men seem to have it simpler in this area because a standard dress suit is easy to wear, acceptable, and not distracting. As a woman, it can get a little more complicated. You want to maintain professionalism, while not compromising your femininity. Avoid wearing bold patterned clothing, and large or noisy jewellery as they can be very distracting! You still want to be yourself, and be aware of what adjustments you may need to make to eliminate and distractions that are within your control in terms of your appearance.

How you show up communicates a message to your audience before you even speak. Does your appearance take away or add to your presentation? As vain as it may seem it is actually an important element in helping to connect with your audience from the onset.

Application:

Get feedback from a speaking coach or professional speaker as to your appearance and whether you need to adjust something to eliminate distractions when you speak.

50.

❧

Don't Let Side Bars Become Slide-Bars

Recently I was listening to a speaker address an audience of about 300 people. I had heard this speaker before so was prepared for his style. However, I was not expecting him to be so unclear and scattered in his presentation. Internally, I kept asking the question, "What's your point?" Although his content was good, his way of communicating was not "sticky". He failed to use anchors to drive home his points (whatever they were) and even worse, continually added sidebar notes to his comments.

As a speaker, my desire and passion is to connect with, transform and empower my audience in some way. What's your desire? What do you want the audience to think, feel and do after hearing you speak?

Before you speak it is important to be clear on what you want your audience to take away. Focus follows clarity and clarity is power! The clearer you are on the points you want to leave with your audience, the more focused you become on what needs to be a part of your message, and what doesn't. This serves as a filter to organize your content.

Too many sidebar comments can create a cluttered speech leaving the audience bouncing back and forth from the main message to the "asides" in their thoughts and emotions. Choose sidebars carefully and limit them to 1 or better yet, none.

Inserting sidebars can quickly take your audience sliding down tracks of thinking that are away from your main points and leave them feeling lost and disconnected from your message. *Don't let your sidebars become "slide-bars"!*

51.

⚖

Use Powerpoint...
Only If Necessary

It's almost expected that if you are conducting a seminar or workshop that you will have a power-point presentation or slides to accompany your message. The danger occurs, however, when you rely too heavily on the slides for your script or direction. Too often presenters end up reading the slides and as a result shift the audience's focus to reading as well.

Power-points were originally designed to be an "aid", however most speakers have forgotten the meaning of this word. The best speakers use slides only to further illustrate a point or to summarize or hit home a point. Excuse my bluntness, but you will find it very difficult to truly *connect* with your audience unless you restrict your slide content and usage. Having said that, when using slides for a webinar, you need a lot more. See my video training called **Effective use of Slides on Webinars!**

If you are in sales, or in corporate settings, presentations may be critical to your bottom line and to your career. I want to challenge you to rethink how you may do your presentation differently.

Don't fall into the trap of thinking it has to be done a certain way in order to be effective. You may discover that an uncommon way may actually yield better results.

One simple tool that most speakers don't use is hitting the "B" button on your keyboard at strategic points during your presentation. The "B" key makes the screen go black, so the audience is not distracted by what's on the screen when you insert a story or make a compelling point. This allows the presenter control over how much focus is given to the visuals or aids and to how much intentional focus on engaging the audience and connecting at deeper levels.

When you spend most of your time looking at your slides instead of your audience you weaken one of the most important goals of public speaking- making a meaningful connection with your audience

Keep in mind that slides were meant to *"support your presentations not become them"*.

Here are three ways that overusing slides can hinder your effectiveness as a speaker:

1. You weaken your personal power to connect deeply with your audience. If you do use slides, only glance at the slide to make sure it is the right one, and speak with your body facing square to the audience, maintaining eye contact.

2. You use it as your script instead of as your guide. This makes the flow less dynamic and usually more boring. If your audience is able to read what you are saying then *one of you is not needed.*

3. You can get lost in the slides if something is out of order or if you run out of time. If you are overly reliant on the slides as your main message, you may end up stumbling to finish strong. Fiddling with technology can be a

huge distraction- remember this saying: *"Anything that distracts, detracts."*

Application:

Evaluate your use of powerpoint slides and create a strategy to use them only when necessary and only slides that enhance and not erode the impact of your presentation.

52.

⌒✑⌒

Your Delivery Will Determine Your Impact

few years ago my family decided to treat me to my favorite food by taking me to a Greek restaurant. I love Greek food so I was really looking forward to the evening. The restaurant was very upscale and clean, however the service ended up being very sloppy and poor. The waitress did not make any effort to connect with us with her eyes or conversation.

When she brought the food it was like she was slapping the plates on an assembly line, and not only that, the food was cold. She had waited too long to bring us the food. Even though the food was actually delicious, how it was delivered had a significant effect on our experience and on whether we would ever return there.

This is the same effect the delivery of your speech will have on your listeners. Even if you have incredible and valuable content, how you deliver that content will profoundly impact your audience's ability to receive and benefit from it.

As you reflect on your delivery method and some ways that you may be able to improve in that area, remember that *If your delivery fails, your content falters, and your audience is left feeling dissatisfied.*

Delivery is often one of the most overlooked areas of public speaking, yet one of the most important when it comes to making an impact.

Application:

Check your awareness quotient and jot down one way you think you can improve your delivery. Record yourself and get feedback on your delivery.

BONUS TIP:

❦

Value Progress Over Perfection

Perfection is an unattainable goal, excellence however is not. As a teenager I fell into the trap of perfectionism thinking that I could execute my life perfectly on my own, never messing up. This kind of thinking led me down a track of becoming addicted to running and snared by an eating disorder called anorexia.

Attaining perfection is a limiting belief. Through a series of choices, a community, and great coaching I overcame the trap and today I value ongoing progress over perfection and as a result, experience tremendous freedom.

When it comes to speaking, *a prepared speech is better than a perfect speech*!

Why? A "perfect speech" usually lacks authenticity, connection, and life. The speaker is often too focused on being perfect, saying things right, and appearing exemplary to make meaningful connections with the audience. When you are focused on yourself, how you are doing rather than on how the audience is receiving, you lose the ability to be relevant and engaging.

When you aim for perfection you often end up coming across as rehearsed, memorized and simply dry, even if you have planned humor. If perfection is a problem you struggle with, I encourage you to seek a coach to help you overcome this trap. Otherwise, you will find yourself struggling to connect authentically, and lack transformational impact.

I find myself repeating this phrase to my clients along their speaking journey and I want to encourage you to memorize it:

"Instead of perfection, aim for connection."

And as you seek to master it, you will find yourself speaking with much greater impact!

About The Author

Lisa Vanderkwaak is a certified executive speaking coach, life strategist, and dynamic speaker who worked in the personal development and spiritual formation arenas since 1989. She is on a mission to equip women to find their voice, speak with increased confidence and clarity and activate them to lead with transformational impact.

Lisa lives in Alberta, Canada with her family.

To contact Lisa to speak at your next event, visit www. lisavanderkwaak.com or to pick up her FREE Speaker Success Toolkit, go to www.Speakingtipsforwomen.com

Other Books by Lisa Vanderkwaak:

Preparing to Speak: 8 Things You Need to Know Before You Step Onto the Platform **(2017) Real U Publishing**

Let the Real You Step Forward Now: 5 Keys to becoming Whole and Experiencing Freedom Everyday **(2018) Westbow Press**

Manufactured by Amazon.ca
Bolton, ON

34269515R00077